IMAGES
of Wales

MILFORD HAVEN
WATERWAY AND TOWN

THANKS TO THEM
MILFORD HAVEN FLOURISHED

Milford Haven's 'Tribute to its Fishermen', a bronze statue by local sculptor, Bryan Hackett, was unveiled on The Rath by the then Mayor, Cllr W.J. 'Bill' Morgan, on 27 September 1992, after being dedicated by the Right Reverend J. Ivor Rees, Bishop of St David's. The words 'THANKS TO THEM MILFORD HAVEN FLOURISHED' summed up the sentiments of all Milfordians.

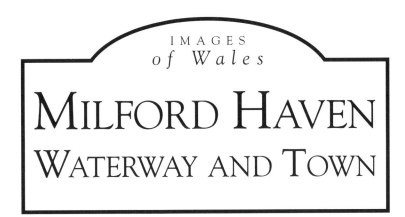

IMAGES
of Wales

MILFORD HAVEN
WATERWAY AND TOWN

Compiled by
Wg Cdr Ken McKay and George Springer
for the Milford Haven Museun

TEMPUS

First published 1999
Copyright © Wg Cdr Ken McKay, George Springer
and the Milford Haven Museum, 1999

Tempus Publishing Limited
The Mill, Brimscombe Port,
Stroud, Gloucestershire, GL5 2QG

ISBN 0 7524 1589 1

Typesetting and origination by
Tempus Publishing Limited
Printed in Great Britain by
Midway Clark Printing, Wiltshire

This 1860s photograph of Hubberston Pill, a major inlet on the Milford Haven Waterway was taken at high tide and shows Hakin in the middle distance on the western shore of the Pill. The building in the foreground is the workshop of the Watson and Wimshurst shipyard.

Contents

The Story of Milford

When Quakers from across the seas,
Saw their homeland in commotion,
Those loyal friends were ill at ease,
And sought to cross the ocean.

Nantucketers these men were called,
And sailed the seas as whalers,
God-fearing, serious folk, we're told,
Though staunch intrepid sailors.

Charles Greville heard about their plight,
And their opinions sounded,
The Haven suited them just right,
So Milford town was founded.

In but few years the whaling ceased,
No use to go on wishing,
The docks were built and trade increased,
As men began a'fishing.

This town became a fishing port,
Though it never was intended,
Fine hake in quantity was caught,
And other schemes were ended.

The trawlers strove for greater hauls,
Fine trips began arriving,
Indeed it now seemed plain to all,
That Milford town was thriving.

From good to bad things took a turn,
Fish trade was now declining,
But through the clouds one could discern,
A glimpse of silver lining.

Whale oil – to fish – and back again?
Fate does take some divining,
How could old Starbuck ascertain,
We'd end up oil refining.

John King

John wrote this poem in 1958 at the beginning of Milford's second oil age – when construction began at the Esso refinery. He was a talented local footballer, became Deputy Head of the Milford Haven Central School and served as Chairman of the Milford Haven Urban District Council. He died in 1991.

Milford and Hubberston Pill around 1810.

Introduction

You can imagine my excitement when asked if I would help prepare a book which would bring into focus the richness and variety in the story of the Waterway and Town of Milford Haven. My co-author, George Springer, was equally enthusiastic. We both help in the Milford Haven Museum which contains thousands of photographs, paintings, pictures and maps. We therefore sought the permission of the Milford Museum Trust to draw from this archive material in preparing this book. They gave their unanimous and willing support.

I am often asked why studying local, national and military history gives me so much pleasure. I suppose, when the result is a book like this, a deep-seated sense of achievement plays a part; but, it goes much deeper than that. Research for my previous books on local history has convinced me that Milford Haven is special. I looked at length for reasons why the history of the area is a story of never ending ups and downs in the commercial well-being of the area. I was also intrigued by unsuccessful early attempts to attract the transatlantic shipping trade. I quickly recognized that the story of the town is inextricably linked with that of its docks and the impressive Milford Haven Waterway from which it got its name.

I questioned if a new dawn had been heralded for Milford by the arrival of the international oil companies in the mid 1900s; but I could not convince myself, even though early euphoria ran very high. The coming of oil to the Waterway was at a time when the local fishing industry was in deep, irreversible decline and this placed the oil bonanza in a position of crucial economic importance. However, the significant oil closures of the past two decades have led me to doubt if oil refining is the final solution to Milford Haven's longer term prosperity. Unemployment now hovers around the 20 per cent level.

My research did, however, strengthen my conviction that, in the long run, it is people and their reactions that really matter. In Milford Haven we find one of the most cosmopolitan populations in the United Kingdom. The Quaker settlers and developers of the late 1700s and early 1800s were joined by fisher folk, one hundred years later, to help support the rapidly growing fishing industry. They came from all around the British coast. Those who arrived with the oil boom of the mid- to late 1900s provided the third major element in the mix. The result is a flexible, multi-skilled, egalitarian group of people who are justly proud of their past and look to the future with hope and optimism in spite of the deep low they see in present local economic affairs.

These factors make me proud of being born a Milfordian and leads to my great pleasure whenever I am called upon to tell the exciting story of the Waterway and Town. However, perhaps the main reason for enjoying this work stems from my belief that an awareness of history is very important. A better understanding of past failures and successes can help in today's planning and hopefully avoid mistakes which might haunt those who follows us.

There is no better time to undertake such an analysis than now, as we approach the millennium. I hope that in doing so you will get added enjoyment from browsing through the pages that follow.

Ken McKay, Honourary Historian, Milford Haven Museum
February 1999

Milford Docks at the end of the Second World War.

One
Early History

This 5ft portion of a mammoth's tusk was found in the early 1930s in deep diggings which were needed for the support pillars of the new Hakin Bridge. Estimates suggest it is 20,000 years old and, if correct, its owner lived some 10,000 years before the retreat of the last ice age and the drowning of the Daugleddau, an event which marked the beginning of the process which produced the Milford Haven Waterway.

When the flooding began, around 8,000 BC, the deep, narrow valley of the Daugleddau was well covered with various forms of vegetation and there were narrow tributaries on both sides. Early erosion predominately involved downward cutting and the deepening of the valley was helped by a slight tilting of the West Wales coast.

Soon afterwards, in geological terms, three things happened. Firstly, the downward erosion was joined by an equally prominent sideways erosion which widened the estuary which secondly began to produce cliffs. Thirdly, offshore islands took shape.

Increased sideways erosion also caused large quantities of gravel, silt and eventually sand to be deposited on the estuary bed. The accumulation continued until these deposits achieved depths of 40 to 50ft in places. Also cliff formation continued and tributaries were widened into what became known as Branches or Pills.

After some thousands of years, we arrived at the deep sheltered Waterway which the Viking visitors of the eighth, ninth and tenth centuries called 'Melr Fyord' (Sandbank Inlet). Phonic developments produced the 'Mellfyth' of the 1200s, followed by the 'Mylford' used by the Welsh historian, George Owen, in the late 1500s. The metamorphosis of the town's name finally arrived at 'Milford', as used by Nelson in his 1802 visit to the town when he described Milford Haven and Trincomalee, in Ceylon, as '…the finest harbours he had seen'.

Even though this is a mid-1950s photograph, it indicates how the Milford Haven Waterway would have looked by the beginning of this millennium. It had become what is known as a 'Ria Coastline' and is undoubtedly one of the jewels in the crown of South Wales. As Shakespear, the Immortal Bard, said: '…how far it is to this same blessed Milford. And by th'way Tell me how Wales was made so happy as T'inherit such a haven.' (*Cymbeline*, Act 3, Scene 2)

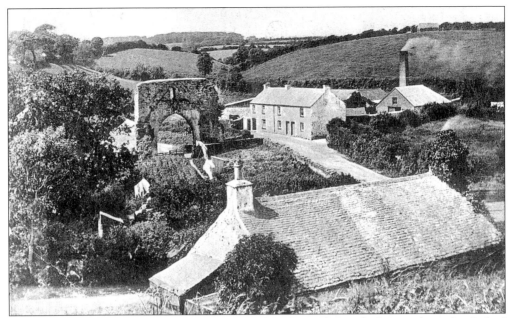

Hubberston Priory was founded in 1170 by Adam de Roche or de Rupe, whose family had Flemish roots. The monks were reformed Benedictines of the Order of Tiron, but the monastery was dissolved by Henry VIII. The original quadrangle structure had buildings on all four sides, but the only remaining major feature is the ruins of the chancel arch. The chimney on the right belonged to the old Priory Sawmills.

St Thomas â Becket chapel, on The Rath, was dedicated in 1180. It was one of three 'beacon chapels' on the north shore of the Haven (no trace remains of the others). Local monks lit a beacon on the seaward side during foul weather to help guide ships to a safe anchorage making the chapel an early, if primitive, lighthouse. It fell into ruin and was used as a store, stable and pigsty until it was restored in the 1930s.

William Hamilton, the grandson of the third Duke of Hamilton, was born in 1730. He was the King's foster brother and uncle of Charles Francis Greville. In 1758 he married Catherine Barlow who owned large estates in Pembrokeshire, including the land on which William eventually built Milford. He was created KCB (Knight Commander of the Order of the Bath) in 1772 while serving as British Ambassador in Naples. In 1791, he married Emma Hart who was both famed and shamed for her amorous relationship with Nelson. Hamilton died in 1803 and, in keeping with his wishes, is buried alongside his first wife at Slebech, near Haverfordwest. (Reproduced from a painting by David Allen)

Charles Francis Greville, a younger son of the Earl of Warwick, was born in 1749. He became MP for Warwick at twenty-four years old and held several minor ministerial and government appointments. He and Emma Hart were lovers before he introduced her to his widower uncle, Sir William. It was Greville who supervized the early building of Milford for Hamilton and succeeded as tenant of the estates when Hamilton died. Charles Francis Greville can therefore be described as Milford's founding father. He died in 1809 and his remains rest in the family vault at Warwick. (Reproduced from a painting by George Romney)

Two
Founding the Town

C A P. LV.

An Act to enable Sir *William Hamilton*, Knight
of the Moft Honourable Order of the Bath,
his Heirs and Affigns, to make and provide
Quays, Docks, Piers, and other Erections ; and
to eftablifh a Market, with proper Roads and
Avenues thereto refpectively, within the Manor
or Lordfhip of *Hubberfton* and *Pill* in the
County of *Pembroke*.

The beginnings of the new town of Milford, on an almost virgin site east of Hubberston Pill, rest
on this Act of Parliament which received Royal Assent on 9 June 1790. It amounts to the
giving of undisputed authority to build a 'proprietary town' – that is to say a town belonging to
Sir William Hamilton.

This 1776 painting by J.R. Attwood shows how Milford Haven might have looked when Charles Francis Greville began his task. In the right foreground is the inlet of Castle Pill and mid-right is Hubberston Pill with Hakin, the then terminal of the Irish Packet trade, nestling on its western shore. The only structures between these pills were the ruins of the St Thomas â Becket chapel and a farm; but this area was to be the site of the new town of Milford. This view looking west gives the impression that the Haven is landlocked because St Ann's Head, its entrance, swings south. The shipping shown is a large part of the British Fleet assembled in the year of the American Declaration of Independence which helps to explain why Nelson was so fulsome in his praise of the Waterway as a possible naval base. (Reproduced from a painting held by the National Museum of Wales)

The first American Quaker whalemen arrived at Milford in August 1792 led by Samuel Starbuck and Timothy Folger, whose portrait is shown here. The original settlement comprised around a hundred people and five whaling ships. Limited whaling began immediately; but, these settlers, even though few in number, were crucial in the early development in the town. The parallel streets are but one example of their influence.

William Rotch Snr, a dominant leader of Nantucket whalemen, failed to persuade the British government, in the 1780s, to accept an American whaling colony at a British port. Milford was considered as a possible location, but Rotch, shown here, favoured Falmouth. He eventually chose Dunkirk, France, with his son, Benjamin, in charge. This colony was, however, forced to close in the aftermath of the French Revolution and Benjamin subsequently joined his cousins, the Starbucks and Folgers at Milford. This provided a much needed boost to the Milford whaling industry.

17

This painting, by American researcher Oswald Brett (1973), shows how Milford might have looked around 1800. The new quay is there and a whale ship is unloading its oil into the Customs Bondage Store – now part of the Milford Haven Museum.

The whale ship *Aurora* carried the Starbuck and Folger families to Milford before setting off on a one-and-a-half-year whaling trip to the southern oceans. This model, made by David Holt, shows the sturdy hull and rigging, the triworks (where oil was extracted from blubber), the capacious hold and the chase boats which carried the harpooners. The whale ship was probably the earliest example of a factory ship.

In 1796 Greville persuaded the Navy Board to build a naval dockyard at Milford. A French Royalist refugee, Jean Louis Barrallier, was sent to supervize the work. He subsequently managed the yard and also became Greville's town planner. This 1812 sketch by Charles Norris shows the launching of the Frigate *Surprise*, one of seven ships launched before the yard was moved to Pembroke Dock in 1814.

The Lord Nelson Hotel, then The New Inn, seen in the Front Street overlooking Hubberston Pill, was opened on 24 September 1800. The architect was Jernigan. Greville felt that the treatment of Irish Packet passengers in Point Street, Hakin, was somewhat crude and hoped his New Inn would perform in 'an improved style'. It was renamed The Lord Nelson after the Admiral's visit with Sir William and Lady Emma Hamilton in August 1802.

The building of St Katharine's, shown here, began in 1801. Greville stated in a letter to Barrallier that he wanted a church of 'duration and elegance'. Some therefore claim its architects were Barrallier and his son; others insist it was the more skilled Jernigan. On completion in 1808 it was designated as a 'chapel of ease' (convenience) in the parish of Steynton. This led to constant disputes over its precise status until Milford was made a separate parish in 1891.

The observatory in Hakin, now in ruins, was one of Greville's more ambitious plans. It was intended to be the centrepiece of a college of science and engineering. Instruments were delivered; but, the selected superintendent, Firminger from Greenwich, never took up post because the plan was abandoned soon after Greville's death in 1809.

The centre section of this building is one of the earliest commercial structures in the town. It was completed in 1797 as the Customs Bondage Store. The two extensions were added around 1806. Its later uses included a fish net braiding and assembly building and a food cold store. The original architect was Jernigan and, appropriately, the building now houses the Milford Haven Museum.

In 1801 Charles Francis Greville gave the American Quakers some land in Priory Road for use as a walled graveyard. Here, there are the graves of generations of Starbucks, Folgers and other Quakers marked only by simple grey stone pillars with their initials and date of death. In 1811 the Meeting House was opened on the site and, even though no descedents of the early settlers now live in Milford, meetings are held every Sunday attended by Quakers from all over Pembrokeshire.

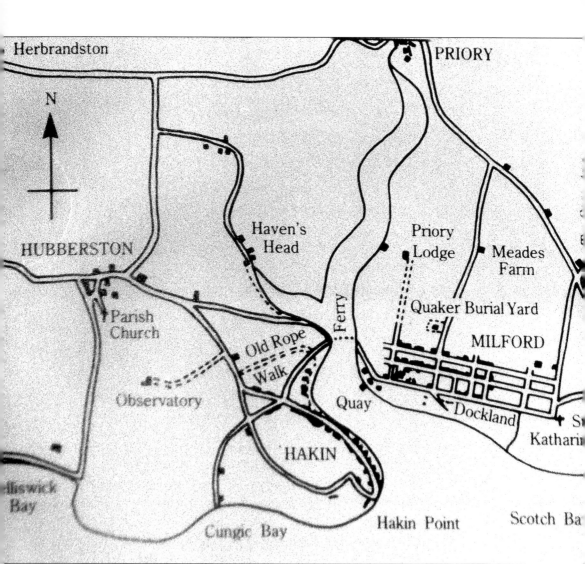

This map shows the town in 1810, immediately after Greville's death and, as can be seen, he had gone some way to achieving his aims. There were about 150 houses and business premises; a new toll road had been built direct from the new town, through Steynton to Haverfordwest and the parallel streets are prominent. A new quay, customs house, hotel and church were also finished. Two temporary defensive emplacements, each built to hold seven guns, had been prepared to defend the dockyard. Milford could now contribute far more meaningfully to what was becoming a busy waterway; but, there was much to be done if lasting prosperity were to be achieved.

Three
The Lean Years

This picture shows the town and Hubberston Pill at high tide in the 1830s. Charles Francis Greville had been succeeded by his brother Robert Fulke Greville, who died in 1824, and was followed by Robert's son, Robert Fulke Murray Greville. Up to 1850, neither showed the same zeal for local development as Charles Francis. In the years following Charles Francis Greville's death much changed in Milford. The Admiralty Dockyard moved to Pembroke Dock in 1814, the Quakers ceased whaling from Milford by 1820 and the Irish Packet service also moved to Pembroke Dock in 1836. Milford had fallen into 'lean years'. (Reproduced from a painting held by the National Museum of Wales)

Robert Fulke Murray Greville felt that the westward progress of the railways, in the mid-1800s, might benefit Milford. He therefore returned calling himself Colonel Greville, complete with the grandiose plans as depicted above by Frederick Wehnert, the Colonel's development advisor with the aim of capturing the Atlantic shipping trade. The plans came to naught, however, because a mainline railway terminal did not come to Milford. The Manchester to Milford Haven Railway was never completed and Isambard Brunel chose Neyland, some 4 miles up the Waterway, as the terminal for the South Wales Railway. By 1863, the Colonel himself had financed and completed a 4 mile, wide gauge, single track railway spur from Johnston to Milford.

This Wehnert drawing from the early 1860s shows Milford and Hubberston Pill seen from the east of the town (The Rath). The Pill looks busy with coastal shipping and there was some shipbuilding and repair work in the small shipyards which had been established. The Colonel's wooden pier can be seen at the bottom of Pier Hill.

This contrasting photograph of the same period shows Milford from the Hakin side, showing Hubberston Pill at low tide. Unlike the Wehnert drawing, the low tide shows how much development was still needed to produce a port of any consequence.

Here is a much more flamboyant Wehnert drawing designed to promote Milford in the 1860s. This explains why it reflects an aura of well-being which was not wholly in keeping with reality; however, the Colonel and Wehnert deserve great praise for their work in the town and port. Colonel Greville died in 1867 and his remains rest in St Katharine's church; Wehnert died in 1871 and he was first buried on the southern side of the church but his body was later moved to the northern side.

In the 1850s, Colonel Greville built this 750ft wooden pier from the cliffs between Milford Beach and Scotch Bay. It had a toll house and hotel and was connected with Hamilton Terrace by Pier Road. It was only a partial success though – some ships in the Irish and local coastal trade used it for loading and off loading, but its main function came to be a tourist attraction.

Some thirty years later, the wooden pier is seen with fishing smacks and small trading ships in the background. The pier had been almost completely destroyed by a closely linked series of heavy storms. Today, only some of the support foundations can be seen at low tide.

27

Colonel Greville gave Milford its first taste of local government – 'The Improvement Commissioners'. However, to ensure his plan was accepted he resorted to a series of local 'sweeteners'. Land for a cemetery at Thornton was offered as well as the wooden bridge in the background of this picture. The bridge crossed Hubberston Pill, had a toll house on the Milford side and was opened in 1859. The sailing vessel in the foreground was typical of those used in the coastal trade; but, more importantly, it sits in the low tide mud of the Pill. The limitations this caused added fuel to the arguments of those in favour of building a floating dock at Milford which was finally begun in 1874.

Colonel Greville's third 'sweetener' was Black Bridge, a similar wooden bridge over Castle Pill in the next inlet east of Hubberston Pill. It was called 'Black' because its pillars were painted with protective bitumen. For the first time there was easy east–west access, at all tides, across the new town. The bridge is now a concrete structure complete with a sluice gate, built in the 1920s.

Castle Hall was originally built in the 1770s as a simple three-storey house by John Zephania Holwell of 'Black Hole of Calcutta' fame (he had been Governor of Bengal and claimed to be a survivor of this ordeal in which 147 men had been imprisoned in a small dark cell). Benjamin Rotch, the Quaker whale merchant, later lived at Castle Hall (1804-1818), and he built the two single-storey extensions and did much to improve the gardens. The Grevilles bought it in 1819 and Colonel Greville added the tower, Ionic pillars and portico. Major Hugh Thomas (later Sir Hugh) lived there after buying the Milford Estate in 1920, and it was, at one time, used as a convent. The building was demolished, around 1939-40, to make way for a road to the new Royal Naval Armament Depot.

In 1872, the broad gauge (7ft) railway spur from Johnston to Milford, was extended to Newton Noyes. The construction involved deep cuttings through rock, as shown in this picture, together with a swing bridge across the entrance to Castle Pill. On completion, the builder, John Milnes, was faced with the immediate task of changing from broad to standard gauge (4ft 8ins), in keeping with the same change being made on the South Wales Railway mainline.

The railway extension ended at this 900ft pier at Newton Noyes, which was designed by J.M. Toler (later the engineer who began construction of Milford Docks). It came into use in 1872 to handle mainly the Irish and coastal trade. This was some sixteen years before Milford Docks were completed.

Four
The Building of the Docks

This view of Hubberston Pill was taken from Hakin a few years before the 'Milford Docks Act 1874' became law and brought into being the Milford Docks Company and authorized: '...the construction of docks and other works in or near Hubberston Pill at Milford...'. This was the sixth major Act of Parliament (following those in 1814, 1851, 1860, 1864, 1872) dealing with docks at Milford. However, this was the first to implement change; the others had not got much beyond the planning stage.

The contract for the building of the docks was awarded to Appleby and Lawton, who had just completed the railway spur to Fishguard and work began on 5 August 1874. Shortly afterwards, the foundation stone (below) was laid near Hakin Point by Edward James Reed CB, MP, Chairman of the Docks Company. It is understood that he is the gentleman, in the dark jacket, standing on the wall above, to the left. Today, the foundation stone is sometimes partially covered by shingle after a high tide as shown here.

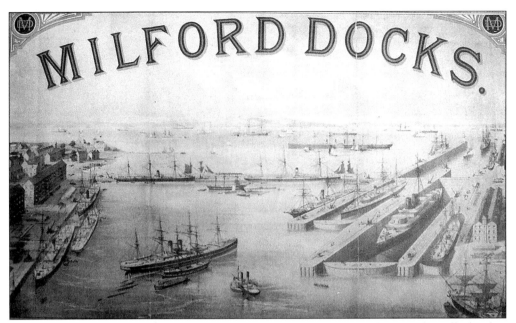

MILFORD DOCKS.

This artist's impression of the early plans show two graving docks – large and small – with a separate entrance lock alongside. The ships shown are mainly of the ocean-going variety underlining that it was intended as a docks catering for the transatlantic trade. The initial plan envisaged a docks which would take two and a half years to complete at a cost £270,000.

A year or so after work began, progress had been made on the dock walls and a fair amount of excavation work had been completed. However, it had already become evident that the task would take more than two and a half years and more money would be needed. The town can be seen in the background and the slipway of Hogan's graving yard (centre right).

The *Great Eastern*, the largest ship then afloat, moved into the partially built Milford Docks in 1875 for a refit. She was initially placed on a grid iron on the Milford side. This episode was used mainly to advertise the large capacity of the new docks. At this stage appreciable work had already been done on the outer wall and the burnt out shell of the Watson and Wimshurst workshop is prominent in the foreground.

This photograph was taken in 1878 from the top of one of the *Great Eastern* paddle housings. She had been moved to the Hakin side of the docks. The bridge (top right) carries the main road over the railway line to Newton Noyes pier. The *Great Eastern* was eventually moved out in the Autumn of 1880, but she remained in the Haven until April 1886, when she went to Liverpool to be broken up.

By 1879 five years of construction had passed, but the docks was far from finished. Then, after conflict with the Docks Company, Appleby and Lawton downed tools and pulled out. Samuel Lake took over and promised to finish by March 1880; however, he gained an extension to March 1881. Lake then overstretched himself financially and stopped work in November 1882 after filing a petition in bankruptcy. Milford began to slip into a deep recession.

The rescue came with the Government sponsored 'Milford Docks Act 1883' which reconstructed the board and revised the capital structure. Work was eventually resumed on 23 January 1886 under S. Pearson and Son – the third builder to be awarded the contract. The docks are seen here just after work resumed.

Changes in the plan were recommended by the new consultant engineer, Alexander Meadows Rendel (later Sir Alexander) and the first, shown here, was a general deepening of the docks to accommodate the ever larger ocean going ships coming off the slipways.

During 1886 and the first half of 1887, rapid progress was made by Pearson and Son and a second deepening was completed. They then hit flooding problems which were overcome by constructing a dam across Hubberston Pill near the bridge accompanied by a culvert which bypassed the docks.

Work also progressed on Rendel's second major change. Because of unsound foundations, previous builders had failed to ensure a watertight seal in the gates of the original lock. This was essential to maintain the water level in the floating dock. Rendel therefore filled in the original lock and modified the larger of the two dry docks for this purpose. He also enlarged the smaller of the dry docks.

Here, in the Spring of 1888, Rendel's new entrance lock and enlarged single dry dock with the docks itself were almost ready for flooding.

New problems arose with rock slippage on the Hakin side of the Pill and this risk being repeated on the Milford side. Second strengthening walls were therefore built. Flooding the basin was further delayed because one of the outer sealing caissons (boat-shaped concrete water sealing structure) refused to be moved. However, as this picture shows, flooding did take place in late September 1888. The work had taken fourteen years of trials and tribulation to complete, at a cost of £1½ million.

One might have expected a transatlantic liner to be the first ship to enter the docks with a blaze of publicity. This was not to be! The first ship, on the 27 September 1888, was the 127 ton steam trawler *Sybil* as seen here. Her catch was sent to Billingsgate, London, where it attracted favourable comment. The Milford Haven fishing industry was born.

By the late 1890s, attempts to attract the transatlantic trade were beginning to sound hollow even though they were still actively pursued. There were negotiations with three Canadian shipping lines and New York and other American owners were also approached. However, these efforts came to nothing and only one scheduled transatlantic liner used Milford Docks – the *Gaspesia* of the Canadian Steamship Line shown above which berthed on 6 December 1898. The promotional poster (right) gives details of this event.

THE

CANADIAN STEAMSHIP LINE.

Shortest Route to Canada.

THE SPLENDID FAST SCREW STEAMER

"GASPESIA"

4000 TONS

WILL BE DESPATCHED FROM

MILFORD to
PASPEBIAC (Chaleur's Bay Gulf of St. Lawrence),

Calling at CHARLOTTETOWN (Prince Edward Island),

On WEDNESDAY, DEC. 7th, 1898.

Goods taken at Through Rates to Quebec, Montreal, and for all interior points of Canada from all points on the Great Western Railway.

Passengers booked at Through Rates to all parts of Canada.

SALOON OCEAN FARES:

To CHARLOTTETOWN AND PASPEBIAC,
From **8 GUINEAS** and UPWARDS,

According to position of State Room and number of berths.

STEERAGE 4 GUINEAS

By 1898, the GWR had extended its rail lines onto Milford Docks. The docks railway station (seen here) was built near Hakin Point but has long since been demolished. It was here that a special group of business men and reporters arrived to board the *Gaspesia* after a record breaking railway journey from London.

Unfortunately, when these passengers arrived, the *Gaspesia* had moved out of the docks and lay at anchor in the Haven. The passengers had to be taken out to her by tender and, apparently,the pressmen were not impressed.

Five
The Fishing Industry

Records from the early nineteenth century indicate that there was some local fishing from both Hubberston and Castle Pills. These Pills were also visited by fishing smacks from Brixton, particularly in the herring season. This supports the earlier claim of the historian, George Owen of Henllys, that Pembrokeshire was '…enclosed with a hedge of herring…'. However, this was a *calling* rather than an *industry*, the advent of which only came with the new docks. Here, in the 1890s, a steam trawler and a sailing vessel are seen in the entrance lock. Very little had been built on the sides of the lock.

The industry grew rapidly and, by 1900, Milford had 65 steam trawlers and some 200 other fishing vessels including sailing smacks and long-liners. This photograph, of that time, shows the paddle trawler *Her Majesty* towing sailing smacks through the lock.

This panoramic view from the late 1890s shows the Fish Market in its early days. Around thirty fish merchants already used the market; but, more importantly, fisher folk from all around the British coast had moved into the new town making Milford Haven one of the most cosmopolitan towns in Great Britain.

Taken from St Anne's Road, Hakin, the view from the very early 1900s shows individually labelled colliery trucks containing quality steam coal in the foreground. Behind them is the old Hakin Wharf with two combined steam and sail driven fishing vessels alongside. Fishing smacks lie at anchor in mid-docks with a number of trawlers alongside the market.

In the early days, vitally important ice was imported from the Norwegian Fjords. In 1890, land was leased for the first local ice factory and a second was built in 1900. Even so, ice still came from Norway for many years to meet peak demands.

Painting and repair of fishing vessels was initially done in the dry dock using a raised structure called a gantry which could take two ships at a time. However, this was both time consuming and expensive and it was superseded in 1909 by a patent slipway built in the main dock. Here fishing vessels could have their bottoms scraped and painted with little fuss and much bigger repairs were also undertaken, as seen here.

The two ice factories can easily be recognized by their tall chimneys, here, in the early 1900s. A a much larger area of the docks was, by this time, occupied by workshops and offices.

W.H. East was one of the leading early fish merchants on the market and these people were employed by him in the late 1890s. We are informed that Mr East is the pipe smoking gentleman in the middle of the front row and his sons are on either side. His descendants still live in Milford Haven.

The original plans for the docks contained two large storage sheds to handle the incoming and outgoing freight from the hoped for transatlantic trade. The Docks Company subsequently joined these unused sheds together for use as a fish market as can be seen here in the late 1890s, when the market was ready for occupation.

Here is the market, ready for one of its first 8 a.m. sales. These were conducted at a hectic pace and the young man with the barrow in the front centre is poised ready to rush the fish, bought and marked by his employer, back to their stand where it would be cleaned and iced in five stone wooden boxes ready for a rapid train journey to London, the Midlands or the North.

In 1907, the Fish Market was lengthened to 950ft and further modified to include a railway loading bay and a covered fish landing area between the opened shed wall and the dockside. These changes speeded up operations even further into what an onlooker might describe as fever pitch.

This is the first in a series of three 1913 photographs showing the trawler *Kirkland* leading a line of trawlers entering the docks just before high tide.

Here trawlers are lined up at the fish market ready for landing their catch. The M 80 *Dartmouth* entered the docks behind the *Kirkland*.

Back on *Kirkland* workmen called 'lumpers' were busily involved unloading the catch on to the market ready for the daily sale which began at 8 a.m.

This panoramic view, just before the First World War, shows that a dozen or more trawlers could be berthed alongside the market ready for unloading.

By the outbreak of the First World War, Milford had one of the finest fish markets in the land. Later, between the wars, it was further extended to 1150ft and an ice delivery runway was built above the front covered landing area along which ice was propelled to a crusher and dispense point in the middle of the now capacious working area.

The growth of the Milford mackerel and herring trade was even more dramatic than that of the trawler fleet. It began in a small way in the late 1890s; but, by 1904, some 200 herring drifters were using the port during the season (April to October). The speed of the turn around was vital and drifters were unloaded at the specially built 400ft landing stage outside the sea wall of the docks. A separate 350ft long herring market was built alongside together with a separate railway loading ramp.

Initially, fish destined for smoke-curing had to be sent elsewhere. However, in 1908, the first large local smoke-house – the old smoke-house shown here – began operations. Four more large smoke-houses and a number of smaller ones were built and operated in and around the docks between the wars and the Milford Kipper became famous.

There are two stages in the preparation of herrings for smoke-curing. The first is sorting, gutting and cleaning and the second involves skewering the 'silver darlings' – the girls' pet name for the herrings – before placing them in the smoke kiln. The 'herring girls' were remarkable ladies. They came mainly from Scotland, the east and south-west coasts. They sang while they worked and spent most of their spare time knitting large sea-boot stockings to supplement their earnings. Many of them married Milford men and founded well-respected local families.

Any account of the contribution of women to the Milford Haven fishing industry would not be complete without mention of the net makers or 'braiding room girls'. A complete trawl had, on average, twelve individual parts which enjoyed colourful names such as 'full belly', 'lower wing', 'square and wings' and 'flappers'. In the beginning these parts were made by women in their homes and then taken to the docks for assembly into trawls. Eventually, the whole process was moved to the braiding rooms on the docks where dozens of skilled women toiled, originally on a piecework basis. They stood at their task for hours on end, the work often causing damage to their joints which led to great pain as they got older – but they rarely grumbled! Yvonne Garnish is seen left in the 1950s, and the group below is from the 1970s. They are, left to right: Mrs Margaret Smith, Trevor Warr (manager of Cosalt), Ira Laugharne, Valerie Davies.

This photograph shows two of the three additional smoke-curing houses near Milford Beach which were built between the wars. It was taken from Marine Villa where the Royal British Legion clubhouse now stands. In 1928 Mr John Warlow of Marine House claimed damages and sought an injunction to restrain the smoke-house owners from causing a nuisance. The case lasted nine days and the judge found that smoke did not cause a nuisance in the legal sense and added that those choosing to live in a fishing port should expect inconveniences of this kind.

The ice factory staff in 1930 were, left to right, back row: Jack Adams, Gilbert Warlow, 'Pop' Vaughan, Harry Venables. Front row: David John, W. Venables, Tommy Vaughan, Eric Becket.

All the filleter of quality fresh fish needed was a very sharp knife, a steady hand and a work bench, improvized from a board and a fish kit (a wooden tub which could hold 12 stone of fish). This skill is seen being exercised, in the mid-1930s, on the Milford fish market stand of A. Wishart and Sons who also operated from Swansea.

This magnificent 32 stone sturgeon (with a roe of 8 stone) was landed in 1933 by the trawler *William Hannah*, skippered by George Thomas. In keeping with tradition, it was offered to the Royal Household before being bought by J.D. Clark for £29.15s. Bob Utting, Harry Roberts, Jack Davies and Hubert Grice are among this group of fascinated market workers.

Skipper James Hewitt and his crew, can be seen on the M 184 *Arthur Cavanagh* (a Castle type trawler) just before leaving for the 1935 Spithead Royal Review of the Royal Navy and Merchant Fleets. The names of Castle ships were drawn from the manning muster logs of the *Victory* and *Royal Sovereign* at the Battle of Trafalgar. The *Milford Countess* represented Milford Haven at the 1937 Review.

Here we see the *Arthur Cavanagh* in between trawlers from Hull and Fleetwood at the 1935 Review. To be selected for appearance in this line was one of the greatest honours which could be awarded to a trawler and its crew.

This oil painting by local artist, T.F. Clayton, shows two Milford trawlers in the heyday of local fishing – *Pheneas Beard* and *Their Merit* – passing at sea. It was originally one of a set displayed in the Fish Trades Restaurant between the wars. It is now in the Milford Haven Museum.

The launch of the *Milford Viscount* took place at Selby in 1947. She was one of the finest equipped trawlers in the country and was skippered by Alex Smith. Unfortunately, she was lost with all hands in a vicious storm in April 1950. The town went into mourning as was always the case when a local trawler was lost at sea.

Here are Milford Docks on 16 November 1955. It had been the home of the fifth biggest fishing port in Great Britain with 130 deep sea trawlers providing jobs, ashore and afloat, for a total of 4,000 people. These two scenes might lead one to conclude that all remained well – the area was still full of workshops and offices and a number of local fishing vessels were berthed at the market. The truth was very different. The decline of the fishing industry in the 1950s had bitten with a vengeance due to diminishing catches, low prices and cripplingly high operating costs. Many knew that the decline was both remorseless and irreversible. Later the problem worsened with the introduction of unworkable EEC fishing regulations.

Even in the mid-1950s this appearence of the Fish Market might have had you believe that all was well. Progress is evident in the form of steel fish containers. Many men appear to be employed and there seems to be an appreciable amount of fish for sale. However, local fish landing statistics reveal the real truth. For the previous thirty years annual fish landings had averaged 40,000 tons. A record 58,000 tons had been achieved in 1946, but this was attributed to under fishing during the Second World War. However, by 1955, the annual catch was down to 25,000 tons and fell to less than 10,000 tons by the mid-1960s.

The Fish Trades Restaurant was in the centre of the Fish Market. The restaurant provided a homely 'tea and wads (sandwiches)' type break for workers from all over the docks. Its first manager, in the early 1900s, was Tom Prickett who was known and loved as 'Doctor Tom' because his famous herbal remedies were always in great demand. Tom was succeeded as manager by his son, Jack, who was followed by Jack's son, Kenny. The restaurant closed in the 1970s.

Here we see Jack Prickett and his son Kenny behind the restaurant counter. Language on the fish market was often very colourful: men hit on the back of a leg by a trolley did not say 'Oh dear'! However, bad language was not welcome in the restaurant. It was 'killed at birth' by Jack's finger being pointed at the offender.

The *Argo of Pembroke*, shown above, was built in the early 1960s by H. Stone and Co. at Brightlingsea for Fred Ingram Jnr of Milford Management, a company associated with Norrard Trawlers. *Argo* was the first Milford trawler to be fitted with a diesel-electric engine and her first skipper was Arthur Harvey. She moved to Fleetwood in the late 1960s and later went on to Aberdeen before being scrapped in the 1980s. The launching, shown left, is that of the *Norrard Star* at R.S. Hayes Yard, Pembroke Dock, in 1956. Her first skipper was Jack Chenery. The *Norrard Star* was special as she was the last Milford trawler to be built around the Haven, and she spent her whole working life at Milford. Most trawlers changed port, name and number – some more than once – during their working life. *Norrard Star* was broken up in 1992.

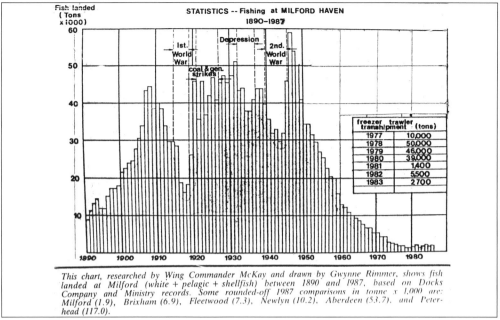

STATISTICS -- Fishing at MILFORD HAVEN
1890-1987

Fish landed
(Tons
x 1000)

freezer trawler transhipment (tons)	
1977	10,000
1978	50,000
1979	46,000
1980	39,000
1981	1,400
1982	5500
1983	2700

This chart, researched by Wing Commander McKay and drawn by Gwynne Rimmer, shows fish landed at Milford (white + pelagic + shellfish) between 1890 and 1987, based on Docks Company and Ministry records. Some rounded-off 1987 comparisons in tonne x 1,000 are: Milford (1.9), Brixham (6.9), Fleetwood (7.3), Newlyn (10.2), Aberdeen (53.7), and Peterhead (117.0).

This bar chart shows, in striking clarity, how the indigenous Milford fishing industry grew, varied in yield and finally collapsed. It spans from 1890 to the late 1980s. By 1990, only a handful of trawlers remained and just over 1,000 tons of fish was landed per year; only one ice factory was left (soon to be demolished and replaced); the Fish Market was a third of its old size and was soon to suffer the same fate; all fish trains and the herring market had long gone; trawler owners, fish merchants, chandlers and engineering works had closed shop; buildings had fallen into disrepair. The once proud docks area looked like an abandoned industrial lot.

In the late 1970s, the docks and market were used by British owned, large, deep sea freezer trawlers equipped with sophisticated fishing aids. They caught large quantities of mackerel mainly for export on refrigerated lorries, trains and reefer ships. Here, trawlers and a reefer ship can be seen in 1979. They ceased operations in the early 1980s after nearly fishing-out the nearby mackerel stocks.

Most fish now landed at Milford Haven comes from powerful French, Spanish and Belgian trawlers like the LO 244 884 *Cassard* shown here. Many claim that these ultra-efficient so-called 'Quota Hoppers' are responsible for damaging overfishing. Nevertheless, some 10,000 tons of fish (with a value of £15 million) was landed at Milford Haven in 1998. However, most of this was transhipped to the trawler's home country in refrigerated lorries.

A new, but much smaller, fish market was built in 1991. It was trebled in size in 1998 and is now home of the Pan European Fish Auction (PEFA) shown here. This is the first of a major computer-based sales system for all fish sold at the Milford Market. Buyers in other countries can use it to compete, over the Internet, with buyers sitting in the market itself. This picture shows, left to right: Hefn Williams (auctioneer), Robert Thomas (network manager) and Mike Jay (general manager) at the Milford Market buyers keypads just before a sale in 1998.

Six
Milford at War

Milford Haven quickly responded to the formation of the Territorial Army. This picture shows the 1st Battalion (TA), The Welch Regiment, (which contained Milford men) at training on Salisbury Plain in 1906. Colonel Roberts (then a Major) is seated on the right.

The Milford Company, 4th Battalion, The Welch Territorial Regiment, pose for a photograph outside the Drill Hall on Charles Street, Milford Haven, in 1908.

A local territorial bicycle patrol at the cross roads, Steynton, at the beginning of the First World War.

The 'Gallant 50', an early group of Milford volunteers, are approaching Milford railway station to join a train to the regimental training grounds in preparation for joining 'Kitchener's Army'. Each recruit was given a packet of cigarettes as a going away present.

Welch Regiment Territorials guarded Black Bridge at the beginning of the First World War. By early 1915, recruiting campaigns became laced with stirring patriotic fervour. One such address, made by a Captain Keates-Wilson on Milford Docks, met with such a high level of success that he was warned not to come again for fear that the docks would be paralyzed by a shortage of labour.

On Saturday 27 August 1917, Private Hubert 'Stokey' Lewis, Milford Haven's Victoria Cross winner, was taken by car with his parents, sisters and brothers on a triumphant journey through the town. The towns folk were ecstatic. Twenty-year-old Private Lewis, 11th Battalion, The Welch Regiment, won his VC on the night of 22-3 October 1916 during a trench raid on the German lines at Machukovo, Macedonia, Greece.

Fund raising was all important to the war effort. Here we see one such campaign, in the First World War, which was centred on the Market Square. The model tank provided a crowd pulling attraction.

Some 80 per cent of the U-boat conflict in the First World War was fought within 100 nautical miles of Milford Haven. A touching tribute was paid to the townsfolk when Admiral Dare, the Naval Base Commander, arranged for this captured German U-boat, U112, to visit Milford Docks so that the people could see the enemy they had helped to defeat. Here we see a visit by a local school.

Private 'Stokey' Lewis VC, is seen here at the laying of the foundation stone of the Milford War Memorial. The base was fashioned by local craftsmen using granite provided by J. C. Ward, the Manager of the Docks Company; this stone had been recovered from the entrance lock to the docks which was originally the large dry dock with a curved base to the walls.

Hubberston Fort, Milford Haven.

BELGIAN MONUMENT, MILFORD HAVEN.

This is a view of Hubberston Fort, which was used by the army for training soldiers during the First World War. In 1914, twenty-four Belgian trawlers with crews and families aboard, fled from Ostend to Milford Haven and stayed for the remainder of the war. In the Second World War it became the American Naval Headquarters with a hospital alongside.

This is the memorial they erected in Hamilton Terrace to mark their appreciation of the hospitality given them. Mr Tom Prickett, of the Fish Trades Restaurant, was a leader of those who helped the Belgians. The vertical pillars around the base were melted down for much needed scrap metal in the Second World War.

This photograph of the Milford Haven Special Constables during the First World War provides an opportunity to review some of the town's most important citizens. They are, back row: P. Hancock, T. Warlow, -?-, J. McKay. J. Lewis, W. Hughes, H. Phelps, W. Davies, T. Thomas. Middle row: Inspector Lewis, G. Baker, E. Brand, T. Hughes, T.D. Morris, J. Howells, T. Mathias, H. Hopton, J. Jones, Sgt Treharne. Front row: L. Davies, F. Lucas, T.G. Hancock, J.B. Gaskell, F. Summers (chief constable), E.E. Carter, W.C. Whittow, F. Johnson, J. Lamb.

The Milford Haven War Memorial, shown here, is one of the finest in Great Britain. It was dedicated on 24 April 1924 by the Venerable Archdeacon of St David's and unveiled by General Sir Ivor Phillips Bart., KCB, DSO. Private Hubert 'Stokey' Lewis VC was also present. Admiral Sir Charles Dare, Milford's wartime Naval Base Commander, donated £215.7s towards the Memorial on the understanding that the names of ninety-one of his officers and other ranks lost in the war would be inscribed on the memorial – this includes the New Zealander, Lt Cdr W.E. Sanders VC.

Milford trawler *Mikasa*, belonging to Jenkersons, left Milford in 1939 to finish conversion for minesweeping duties. Over fifty of Milford's best trawlers were requisitioned for naval duties in the Second World War.

This picture shows nineteen-year-old Albert Gwilliam CGM, the town's first hero of the Second World War, being honoured by the presentation of an inscribed plaque by Cllr Meyler, Chairman of the Milford Haven Urban District Council accompanied by Cllr Ivor Phillips, Headmaster of Albert's old school, the Central School. Albert won the Conspicuous Gallantry Medal when serving on HMS *Exeter* in the Battle of the River Plate on 13 December 1939.

Many Milford girls, joined by others, served in the Women's Royal Naval Service during the Second World War. Two members are shown here; standing is Milfordian, Mary 'Molly' Phillips.

The Dale Roads anchorage in the Milford Haven Waterway was an important convoy assembly centre which brought the Second World War very close to those living in the area. Convoy briefings were held at South Hook Fort or the Lord Nelson Hotel. Between 1939 and 1945 a total of 60 million tons of shipping joined convoys at Dale Roads. Most were destined for the Western Approaches, but a few sailed the punishing journey around the North Cape to Russia.

Twenty-six Dutch minesweeping trawlers helped keep the Milford Haven Waterway clear of German mines between late 1940 and mid-1943. The top picture shows the minesweeper *Gerbordina Johonna* in the Haven in 1942. Her Dutch crew is shown in the lower picture. They boarded with local families and a number of these young, handsome Dutch sailors married Milford girls.

This German DO 18K, a push/pull seaplane, is seen laying mines near Dale Roads on a moonlight evening in 1941, just before a convoy was due to sail. The mines were dropped in pairs – one magnetically triggered and the second acoustically (sound) triggered. This activity continued until late 1943. (Reproduced from a painting by Bob Rickard)

Here we see the body of a Dutch sailor being carried out of their adopted church, St Peter's, in 1943. Like other military casualties in the area, burial took place in the War Graves section of Milford Haven Cemetery at Thornton. St Peter's church suffered a sad fate when, in 1994, it was accidentally burnt down.

The popular HMS *Adventure* is shown here. She was a defensive minelayer and laid many thousands of mines, which were assembled at the Royal Naval Armament Depot, Milford Haven, all around the British coast. To give some idea of the magnitude of the mine depot's task, one should note that they assembled 186,000 buoyant impact mines (Mk 17) during the war as well as many more sophisticated sea mines including those designed for airborne delivery.

HMS *Adventure* intercepted a German blockade runner on 12 April 1943. Blindfolded prisoners, shown here, were taken ashore at the mine depot jetty and loaded onto a guarded bus for conveyance to an interrogation centre and then a prisoner of war camp.

In 1934, the Council of Imperial Defence decided that the concentration of key munitions and defence installations in South East England was vulnerable to air attack. Out of this came the decision to builtd Royal Naval Armament Depots at both Castle Pill, Milford Haven, and Trecwn in North Pembrokeshire. Building started in 1935 and was finished in the winter of 1939-40; this included extensive strengthening of the old jetty on the site. Here are two of the lengthy storage tunnels which were dug into the hillside at Castle Pill and the railway lines feeding them.

In all, six fast minelayers were built during the Second World War. They were loaded at the mine depot at Milford Haven before undertaking their dangerous missions off the approaches to key enemy coastal areas including entries to main ports. They were fast (reaching speeds of 40 knots) with capacious holds and were used in supply runs from Gibraltar to Malta during the siege of the George Cross Island. Here we see one of these impressive ships HMS *Apollo* just after the war.

On 25 April 1943 two Landing Craft Guns (LCGs 15 and 16), on passage from Holyhead to Falmouth, foundered in a fierce storm off the Pembrokeshire coast. Of the seventy-five men on board, only three survived. Many of those killed are buried in the War Graves section of the Milford Haven Cemetery. A special and moving tribute has been placed alongside these graves by their Landing Craft Gun comrades.

Throughout the first half of 1944, Milford Docks and Wards Yard, just to the east, were kept busy repairing, refitting, modifying and equipping landing ships and craft of all kinds ready for the invasion of Normandy. Here we see a Landing Ship Tank being refitted in Milford Dry Dock.

Seven

The Town of Milford Haven

Point Street was one of the earliest built-up streets in what became the town of Milford Haven. It ran from Lower Hill Street, Hakin, to Hakin Point. Parts of some of the houses – particularly chimneys – are reminiscent of early Flemish influence (from the twelfth to the fifteenth centuries). In the late 1700s the street housed a number of inns serving the Irish Packet trade. Unfortunately, in the early 1950s, it was demolished to make way for improvements to the docks which were never fully realized. Consequently, Milford Haven lost an important part of its architectural heritage.

Here, supplies are being delivered to Farrows General Produce Store in Charles Street in the very early 1900s. Mr Farrow is standing by the delivery cart, with his baker, the delivery boy and a shop assistant.

The laying of the foundation stone of the 'Bethel' (The Mission and Welfare Centre, British and Foreign Sailors Society) in 1907 by Mrs David Lloyd-George (the lady in black, right, holding the sheet of paper). The building, in Charles Street, was paid for by John Cory, the Cardiff shipping magnet, and it was opened in 1908. It became a small shopping mall in the late 1980s.

By the early 1900s, Hamilton Terrace had been laid out with double pavements and long grass lawns on the seaward side. This was the 'Front Street' of the early American Quaker whaling developers and most of the houses shown were originally occupied by leaders in that enterprise, in keeping with their desire to have simple, yet solid houses overlooking the sea.

This picture shows the junction of Lower Hill Street with the then Spikes Lane, around 1900. The Hakin sub-police station was halfway down Lower Hill Street. In 1857 the Milford Haven main police station and lock-up was opened in Fulke Street, but was moved to the corner of Trafalgar Road and Dartmouth Street in the early 1900s where it was joined by the Sessions Hall. It now occupies a site in Charles Street.

Charles Street, originally Middle Street, is shown here with the Market Square and market self-evident, *c.* 1910. Both were among the features called for in the 1790 Hamilton Act. The market had a statue of a bull on top of its wall and a Victorian horse drinking trough facing the pavement. The bull mysteriously disappeared before the market building became a cinema (The Astoria) between the wars. The drinking trough is now outside the Town Hall and the cinema became a bingo hall in the late 1970s.

Hadfield's fancy goods store occupied a site on Charles Street in the early 1920s. This was a time when most shopping by townsfolk was done in Charles Street where a full range of goods was on sale. Milford Haven was prosperous at that time and shop sites in Charles Street were in great demand; many were extensively renovated when they changed hands.

Another very popular Charles Street shop was Foster Powell's seen here as it was between the wars. After the Second World War, another storey was built on top as part of a large new development which closed off one of the roads to Hamilton Terrace. This shop was one of the favourites of young people, particularly at birthday and Christmas times.

The Ind Coope brewers drayman, Alfred Barrett, stands by his delivery dray behind the Kimberly public house where the horses were stabled in the 1920s. In many ways this is a family photograph, showing Alfred's children and workmates.

This 1931 picture shows the 1887 iron Hakin Bridge and its toll house which had replaced the original 1859 wooden variant built by Colonel Greville. The iron bridge and toll house were subsequently demolished and replaced by a third version, a reinforced concrete bridge.

The Hakin Bridge tolls (a halfpenny per person and sixpence per cart) were increasingly resented – particularly by those living in Hakin. The Urban District Council (MHUDC) therefore abolished them on 2 October 1909. This was marked by the issuing of commemorative mugs to all Hakin schoolchildren. The parade, seen here, was about to start on 'Captain James' Hill' before crossing the bridge for a celebratory address and then marching back up St Anne's Road.

This picture, from early 1933, graphically illustrates the construction of the new reinforced concrete bridge (costing £45,000) which was well underway and the iron bridge alongside which was still being used. The toll house had, at this time, yet to be demolished. The opening of the new bridge was scheduled for 12 October 1933, but was cancelled owing to the sudden death of the Town Clerk (T.G. Williams). The Hakin folk held their own celebration on 25 November 1933 which included souvenir mugs for children.

MHUDC improvement plans in the inter-war years provided Milford with the swimming pool on The Rath (at a cost of £11,000). It opened in 1939 ready for maximum use by servicemen and women in the Second World War. Patronage began to decline in the early 1970s, and when the heated indoor swimming pool opened at the Meads Sports Centre in 1973, swimmers at The Rath Pool fell to a mere trickle and it was closed in 1987 amid much local sadness. It was replaced by a terraced water gardens area which was opened by the Prime Minister, Margaret Thatcher MP, in September 1990.

The inter-war MHUDC programme had included the electrification of the town in 1926 – the first in Wales – a new sewerage system in 1930 and the ambitious Prescelly Water Scheme in the mid-1930s. There was also the new Town Hall, centre, in the 1970s. The foundation stone was laid by Major Gwilliam Lloyd George MP in 1938. It was to be officially opened on 31 August 1939 by his illustrious father, David Lloyd George MP, but he was kept in London by the worsening crisis which led to the Second World War. Like the reinforced concrete bridge, the new Town Hall was never officially opened.

Milford Haven's response to the Nonconformist Revival of the late 1800s and early 1900s was impressive. Three large new chapels were built and opened: the Baptist chapel on North Road in 1879, the Methodist chapel in Priory Road in 1902 and the Tabernacle chapel in Charles Street shown here after its opening in 1910. These three, together with the other churches and chapels which were already thriving, played key roles in the spiritual, social and cultural well-being of the town.

The two oldest churches in the town of those days go back to the 1100s. These were the, then derelict, St Thomas â Becket 'Beacon Chapel' on The Rath (see p. 13) and St David's church, Hubberston, shown here.

There were a number of privately owned schools in Milford in the early 1800s. Churches and charitable organizations expanded this range. Successive Government Education Acts further consolidated the coverage and new school buildings were completed from the 1850s to after the Second World War. North Road Board School, together with the school house and gardens, is seen here in the early 1900s.

The original County School (later to become the Grammar School) was opened in 'Marine Villa' – now the Royal British Legion – in 1896. It moved to a new building in North Road in 1901 which was much enlarged in 1937. The last move, in 1964, was to the new building in Steynton Road shown here where the school was further enlarged and joined by the Central Secondary Modern School to become a new comprehensive in 1988.

In 1909, the Town Council opened the Milford Fire Station in Dartmouth Street, equipped with a top of the range, horse-drawn Shand Mason steam pump. In 1925, they acquired the first-class Stanley vehicle shown above. The lower picture shows them with their new Leyland FK7 Cub after moving behind the new Town Hall in 1939. The men themselves were *retained* part-timers but on the left is Chief Officer Matt Acornley, the first professional, salaried man to be employed. The move to Yorke Street came in November 1966 where they now function as part of the Mid and West Wales Fire Brigade.

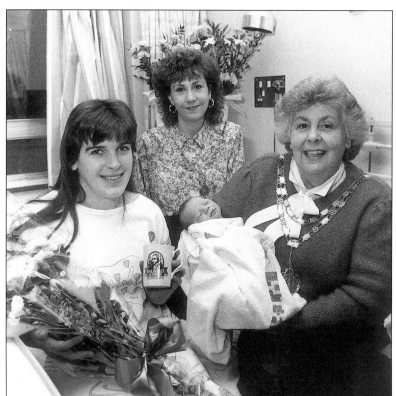

The Milford Haven Bicentennial celebrations were spread over the whole of 1990. Celebratory mugs were given to all children. The first of these was given by the Mayor, Cllr Sheila Russell, accompanied by her consort (her daughter Christina), to Andrew the baby son of Mrs Beverly Mathias on 11 January 1990.

The guest of honour on the actual 200th birthday, 9 June 1990, was Princess Alexandra, shown here talking to Ron Ramage one of the Round Tablers who helped with crowd control. Her husband, The Rt Hon. Angus Ogilvy, can be seen talking to invalids behind the barrier.

Milford Haven knows how to enjoy an important event. The main shopping street, Charles Street, assumed a festive air on 9 June. Children were offered rides on the free roundabout as shown here. Thousands of townsfolk and equal numbers from further afield joined in the fun which ended with a firework display in the late evening organized by the Young Lions.

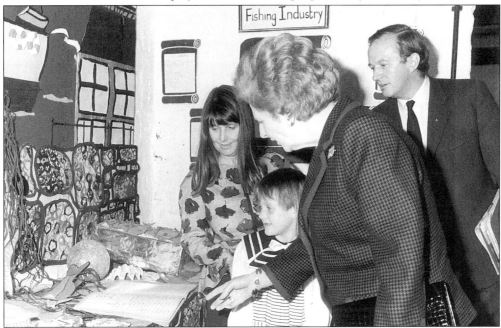

Each of the Milford Haven junior schools produced colourful contributions to an historical exhibition to mark the town's Bicentenary in 1990. It was opened, in the museum, by Princess Alexandra on 9 June and closed by Margaret Thatcher during her visit to the town in September – one of the last civic visits she made as Prime Minister. Here we see her with, left to right: Sonnia Stevens (a teacher from Waterston School), Sarah Mayne (pupil) and David Hunt MP, Secretary of State for Wales.

Charles Street, Hamilton Terrace and The Rath underwent an extensive facelift in the early 1990s. This is the enhanced Market Square end of Charles Street, further bedecked for a civic function.

With supertanker *Alexandros* behind them, the entrants line up for the start of the 1991 Tall Ships Race at Milford Haven. They are, left to right, the Polish barquentine *Iska*, the topsail schooner *Malcolm Miller* and the 182ft Dutch schooner *Eendract*.

The race was started by The Duke of York on the Royal yacht *Britannia*. Here we see him inspecting the competitors moored in the newly prepared marina, Milford Docks. He is on the right of the group on the jetty with his hand on the deck of a boat.

The topsail schooner *Sir Winston Churchill*, the Polish brigantine *Henryk Rutkowski*, the brig *Astrid* and the Irish brigantine *Asgard ll* sail past *Britannia* at the start of the race just outside St Ann's Head on Sunday 21 July 1991.

The 'Milford 2000' plan, launched in 1990 with EEC financial backing, was designed to convert the then semi-derelict docks into a marina, a modern industrial and commercial complex and provide quality domestic accommodation. A great deal has been achieved and many say it is now a pleasure to walk around the area. A simultaneous scheme, shown here, was the building of the fourth Hakin Bridge because the third bridge had been hit by what is termed 'concrete cancer'. The new bridge was planned by Ironbridge Estates and built by Tarmac construction.

The picture above shows both the new building and demolition almost complete. In the background is the Torch Theatre which began life in 1977. The lower picture shows the completed new bridge which was to be opened by Ron Davies, Secretary of State for Wales, on 22 June 1998. However, he was unable to attend so the job was handed to the Mayor of Milford Haven, Cllr Anne Hughes. Peter Hain, Minister of State at the Welsh Office, witnessed the ceremony.

Another major development in the 'Milford 2000' plan was the building of a large shopping park beyond Hakin Bridge and between Haven's Head and the railway station, which itself is scheduled for improvement. The complex was planned to be spacious with ample car parking available. Sited between the two main parts of the town – Milford and Hakin – the complex has already revolutionized the pattern of shopping of the townsfolk and many travel from much

further afield to take advantage of the facilities. A funicular railway/lift arrangement is being considered to connect the complex to the Torch Theatre and Milford's traditional main shopping centre in Charles Street. This would go a long way towards raising Milford Haven's status as a shopping and cultural centre.

This aerial photograph, taken while the Tall Ships were assembling in mid-July 1991, not only underlines the massive amount of work which was needed to prepare for this prestigious event, but also gives a clear indication of the development potential of the surrounds of the docks, much of which had been realized by the late 1990s, with more planned.

Eight
The Second Oil Age

The Esso Refinery at Herbrandston began operations in July 1960 and was opened by HRH The Duke of Edinburgh on 3 November 1960. Here, he is unveiling the tribute plaque (now in the museum) to the 3,500 men who built the refinery and those who would operate it. It formally marked a transformation in the story of Milford Haven. Local people came face-to-face with a completely new challenge and they responded in a remarkable way. The growth was phenomenal. The British Petroleum terminal opened at Popton in April 1961; Regent, now Texaco, at Rhoscrowther in September 1964; Gulf at Waterston in August 1968; Amoco, now Elf Acquitaine, at Robertson in September 1973. Milford Haven had become the largest oil port in Europe.

Worldwide interest was being shown in the oil port of Milford Haven even before Esso came online, as can be seen by this visit of foreign journalists to the Esso construction site in December 1958. They were accompanied by councillors and officers of the Milford Haven Urban District Council who fully supported the oil companies.

The Esso jetty is seen here with a tanker alongside soon after the refinery began operations.

The British Petroleum jetty with the Norwegian tanker *Tharald Brovig* alongside, connected to the pumps feeding crude to their refinery at Llandarcy, Swansea, in the mid-1960s.

The *Esso Pembrokeshire* (81,000 tons deadweight) being berthed at the BP jetty on 6 November 1961 with three Cory tugs in attendance.

If we include the Pembroke oil fired power station and the Cleddau Bridge, building activity around the Milford Haven Waterway in the quarter of a century after the start of the Esso refinery was without equal in West Wales and probably rarely equalled elsewhere. The speed of building was phenomenal. The picture above, taken 15 July 1971, looking south with Esso in the background, shows the initial clearance of virgin farmland at Robertson for the Amoco refinery; the lower one, taken in November (four months later) and looking north, shows the amazing progress already made on this site.

Tom Goddall and Herbert Roach checking manifold and control valves on the Gulf Oil liquid petroleum gas storage spheres in 1978.

All oil refineries carry out periodic and expensive refit and modification programmes. This is the heart of the distillation processing units at the Gulf Refinery and shows the heat exchangers being cleaned and repaired in 1980.

The Very Large Crude Carrier (VLCC) *Esso Scotia* is seen unloading at Milford Haven in the early 1970s. Between the mid-1970s and mid-1980s, the number of VLCCs using Milford Haven dropped steadily because the North Sea fields became the main source of crude entering the port and this could be carried more economically on smaller tankers.

Milford Haven is shown here nestling in the middle of an impressive refinery complex in the late 1970s. Esso is just off picture but the Amoco, British Petroleum, Texaco and Gulf jetties can be seen, as can the Conservancy Board jetty, Milford Docks and the piers at the, virtually closed, Ward's Yard and the Royal Naval Armament Depot (RNAD). Things were soon to change. Esso closed in 1983, British Petroleum in 1985 and Gulf in 1998: all the result of worldwide over production in petroleum products. The RNAD closed in 1991.

Without doubt, the oil industry has been a blessing to the economic well-being of the area and these companies' support of local charities and worthy causes has been without equal. Nevertheless, there have been problems, though thankfully few, over their forty-year life in Milford Haven. There was a very large fire at the Amoco plant in the mid-1980s and this picture shows a big fire following an explosion at Texaco in early 1994. On both occasions the fire service and refinery staff acted promptly and effectively to contain the blazes.

The *Sea Empress*, shown here, ran aground when entering the Milford Haven Waterway in early 1996 spilling 72,000 tons of crude oil which polluted much of the Pembrokeshire coast, coastal waters devastating both bird and sealife. This disaster is often erroneously linked with a similar, but much smaller incident in October 1978 involving *Christos Bitas*. This tanker was not entering the Haven but passing outside while *en route* from Rotterdam to Belfast.

An unfortunate consequence of towing the still leaking *Sea Empress* into Milford Haven was that it increased the pollution inside the Waterway. Crude oil even spread into Milford Docks and affected its famous swans. This picture shows thick crude at Hakin Point.

The *Sea Empress* disaster attracted worldwide media attention, but this had largely disappeared when the real work – the clean up – began. The local authorities and the oil companies are to be congratulated for what has been described as one of the best planned and most effective clean up operations in the history of oil spills. Here we see a team on one of the larger beaches; their efforts ensured that South Pembrokeshire was cleaned and ready for the summer season.

Nine
It's People That Matter

Any discussion about people in West Wales towns like Milford Haven quickly leads to talk about children and hence schools and education. It is therefore appropriate to begin with this group of well dressed, bright looking pupils at the North Road Board School in 1895. The school was so called because it was opened in 1877 by the Steynton School Board which itself was formed soon after compulsory education was introduced by the Education Act of 1870.

In the first half of the 1900s most entertainment was home grown with churches and schools prominent in organizing these activities. Here we see the April 1910 cast of St Katharine's Operatic Society production of *Caractacus – First English King*. There were many active amateur dramatic and operatic groups in the town with a new production from one or other of them almost every month.

The cast enjoyed a 'second bite of the Caractus cherry' by producing this float for the annual carnival held later that summer. The Milford Haven annual carnival, now organized by the Round Table, has always been looked upon as one of the best in West Wales.

This photograph of a group of male pupils at the Milford Haven County Intermediate School was taken in 1910, nine years after it had moved from Marine Villa to North Road. The original school was opened as a result of The Education Act of 1887 which was designed to provide the secondary education needed to prepare pupils for the University. They are, left to right, back row: Walter Galvin, Harold Bowen, Barclay Foster, Oliver Little, William Hughes, John Davies, Maurice Miller, Hubert Day. Middle row: Guy Young, Gilbert Skone, Harry Roberts, Charles Payne, Walter Kilby, William Payne, Victor Cleaver, William Cole, Owen Limbrick. Front row: Russell Lowther, Arthur Oswald, Bert Lowther, William Gibby, Percy Kilby, Harold Heath, Sanders Lambswood, Tom Lewis.

The Priory Mission Sunday School was a thriving institution as the staff and pupils, shown here, illustrate in 1910. The school was at the top of Priory Hill – now renamed Cromwell Road – which leads down to the ruined Hubberston Priory. The mission building was demolished after the Second World War to make space for road improvements leading to the new Howarth Close estate.

During both world wars, areas of land all over the country were used for vegetable growing thereby helping the 'Dig for Victory' campaign, and Milford was no exception. Here, the Sunday school pupils of St Peter's church are preparing the front lawns for planting during the First World War.

One of the most popular means of fundraising to help worthy causes is to organize a fête or hold a raffle. Here we see two stalls at a typical church fête of the early 1900s. It was held in the grounds of Hamilton House, a venue often used for this purpose. These gardens were consecrated as the Memorial Gardens after the Second World War, complete with beautiful flowers boarders and open for all to wander around at all times.

In the early 1900s, much sought after apprenticeships were available all around the Milford Haven Waterway the most popular being at the Royal Naval Dockyard, Pembroke Dock. There were also many such opportunities in and around Milford Docks. This 1908 group of apprentices were at the Francis Ship Building and Repair Yard, Castle Pill.

The townsfolk of Milford Haven played a key role in both world wars. This concert was held in the Trafalgar Institute in 1919 to mark the closing of the war time Naval Base and pay tribute to those who served there.

Between the wars, a favourite form of enjoyment for all groups, including Sunday schools, was a charabanc trip to one of the many local beaches or beauty spots. Here, St Katharine's Mothers' Union wait in a charabanc outside the vicarage before leaving for Llanstephen in 1927.

This photograph shows a team of the Milford Haven Urban District Council road repair workers in the 1920s. They are, left to right, back row: -?-, Mr Mathias, Mr Devonald. Middle row: Mr H. Evans, Mr Bevan, Mr Warlow. Front row, kneeling: Mr J. Evans, Mr Laugharne (who also drove the steam roller).

Hakin National School, in the parish of Hubberston, is seen here in 1929. The foundation stone of this National (Church) School was laid on 12 April 1855 by Mrs Clarke, the wife of one of Colonel Greville's friends. The colonel donated the site, and building costs came mainly from local donations. The Headmaster, Harold Lewis, is on the right and he could be described as Milford Haven's 'Mr Music'. He led high calibre adult choirs and an orchestra, and taught many young people to play musical instruments, maintaining their interest through a youth orchestra. Added to this, he was involved with children's choirs. He had a significant impact on local music.

If you were to ask Milfordians who went to school in the 1920s and '30s where their parents bought their school clothes, at least one in four would reply 'Ocky White'. Here is his delivery van in the early 1920s. In the 1930s he established a shop in Haverfordwest which became one of the largest stores in West Wales. Even so, he continued to live in Hakin and retained a small shop in North Road, Milford Haven.

The 'concrete' Hakin Bridge was opened in 1933. However, in the month before the opening, Milford Haven experienced a striking example of 'People Power'. Doubts spread about the strength of the new bridge when compared with its iron predecessor. To satisfy the doubters the builders arranged for eight steam rollers to cross the bridge in close convoy before other vehicles were allowed to use it.

This Hakin (west side) team was employed to open and close the manually operated dock gates. Those identified are, left to right, back row: Chris Smith, Reg Farmer, George Hyatt, Leslie Hancock. Front row: Elliot Payne (standing), Henry Mathias, -?-, Jim Phillips Snr, 'Bosun Jack' Lewis, Jim Phillips Jnr.

The various missions to seamen played key roles in the story of Milford Haven; never more so than during the two world wars. Miss Wood (left) and Miss Watson were the superintendents of The Royal National Mission to Deep Sea Fishermen, Lower Charles Street (now the offices of Edwards the Printer).

The Milford Athletic Football Club in the 1925/6 season. They include, left to right, back row: Victor Clever (second), Stanley Brown (fourth), Cecil Clark (seventh). Middle row: Ivor East (second), Victor Banner (third). Front row: Sid Price (centre).

This 1936 line-up of the Milford Haven County School soccer team is notable because the team began the school's run of more than ten years without defeat. They are, left to right, back row: Wilfred Warlow, Derek Mclean, Benny Russell, Billy Rees, John Petrie, Norman Avery, Elwyn Packman, Kenny Evans. Front row: John King, Billy Johnson, Winston Williams, Cyril Morris, Roger Finney, Mr Cliff Davies (sports and geography master).

The youth of Milford were always spoilt for choice when it came to youth organizations. Scouts, Guides, Cubs, Brownies, Church Lads' Brigade and later the various military youth organizations could be numbered among those available. The 6th Milford Haven Company of Guides, based at the Central School, is seen here in the mid-1930s.

The 1939 Milford Haven County School cricket team is seen here outside the wooden changing rooms on the school playing field at Marble Hall, about half a mile from the school itself. They are, left to right, back row: Norman Gilbert, John King, William Sweeney, William Lewis, Glyn Jones, John Medway, Cliff Davies (geography and sports master). Front row: Eric White, Roger Finney, Wally Walters (captain), William Rees, Morgan Garrett. Sitting at the front: Ronnie John and Henry Lewis.

The Milford Haven Urban District Councillors, under the chairmanship of Cllr Ivor Phillips (Headmaster at Central School), assembled outside the new Town Hall in 1940. On the right of the front row is Mr Howarth, the highly qualified and very efficient Town Clerk who had, only a few months earlier, been successful in resisting an attempt by the Royal Navy to requisition the building.

Milford Haven was one of the first towns to form a branch of the British Legion, soon after the First World War. At the Branch Annual Dinner, in 1935, were, left to right, standing: B. Burley, T. Taylor, C. Toms, R. Finney , S. Alford , Major Stokes, H. Calderwood, V. Thomas, J. Hunt, M.M.R. Elder, A. Kennedy, H. Stephens, R. Joyce DCS, B. McKay, V. Cleaver. Seated: G. Roberts, G.S. Belton, H. Smith, H.W. Lewis VC, Lady Haig, Mrs Stokes, H. Sheriff, B.H. Johns, T.V. Williams, W. Austin.

This group of construction workers were involved in clearing the site for the construction of the Royal Naval Armament Depot (mine depot) at Milford Haven in 1936. Included are: Frank Hastings, in the middle of those seated (he later joined the Royal Marine Commandos and was killed in action in Italy in 1944); the man with his arm around Frank is Matt Poole and standing to the left is Edwin Price; the man in the cab is Matt's brother Tom Poole.

During the Second World War, and for decades afterwards, the mine depot was a major employer in the Milford Haven area. In 1941 the Canteen Staff were, left to right: Mrs Joyce French, Mrs Ruby Sandy, Miss Llewellyn (supervisor), Mrs Esme Howell, Mrs Olive Liddle.

The Queen visited Pembrokeshire in August 1955 and spent some time at Milford Haven. She is seen here, under the decorative awning outside the Town Hall, accompanied by Colonel G.T. Kelway, Deputy Lord Lieutenant of Pembrokeshire, with Prince Philip and Vivian Lewis, Chairman of the Milford Haven Urban District Council, in the immediate background.

Local amateur groups in the form of orchestras, choirs, operatic and dramatic societies played an important part in the lives of those living in Milford Haven. This shows a very popular smaller orchestral group 'The Astorians' in 1951. They are: Eric Robson, Tommy Rowlands (accordions), Eric White (violin), Richy Narbett (piano), Billy Hughes (drums).

This picture, taken on on 4 October 1960, demonstrates only one of the many skilled and semi-skilled jobs which were then available at the Royal Naval Armament Depot. The men, left to right: Fred Oughton, Bill Thomas and Jimmy Owen, are shown testing an assembled mine casing for leaks.

Milford Haven has always looked after its old folk. Here we see Dorothy Miller (left), one of the leading lights in fund raising for pensioners, at the opening on Saturday 23 June 1962 of The Haven Club, Pill Fold. She was accompanied by Dillwyn Miles, Desmond Donelly (the local MP) and Rose Rolston.

The Royal family, and their hosts, on the dais at the Gulf Refinery, 10 August 1968, when Her Majesty Queen Elizabeth II, accompanied by Philip, Duke of Edinburgh, Prince Charles and Princess Anne, officially opened the Waterston Oil Refining complex. The company, the people of Milford Haven and indeed Pembrokeshire at large, took pride from the fact that this was the first time that so many members of the Royal Family had graced a function like this with their combined presence.

The combined schools and Milford Haven Operatic Society choirs were joined outside the Town Hall by the Haverfordwest Male Voice Choir on the Bicentenary (9 June 1990) to sing the Town Anthem – *Thou Blessed Haven* – composed by a distinguished son of Milford Haven, Edmund 'Wally' Walters.

Mr Stephen Griffith and Mrs Kay Allen, Clerk of the Milford Haven Meeting leading local Quakers, are seen presenting the Milford Haven Panel, one of seventy-seven in the Quaker International Tapestry, to Mrs Joyce Harries the Mayoress in the second half of 1990, the Bicentennial year.

To mark the 'American Connection' with the story of Milford Haven, Mr and Mrs William Rotch from Milford, New Hampshire, United States, (shown above) visited the town. William, a descendent of Benjamin Rotch, the leading whale oil merchant at Milford in the early 1800s, spoke eloquently from the Town Hall steps at the impressive Bicentenary civic ceremony on the morning of 9 June 1990.

The United States also paid tribute to Milford Haven's Bicentenary by sending their frigate, USS *Pharris* FF1094, on a courtesy visit in June 1990. Here we see the Bicentennial Queen, Sarah Canning, receiving a bouquet from the captain, Commander Jeff Davidson, at a 'Welsh Night' organized for the crew. On the right are Councillor and Mrs Eric Harries the Mayor and Mayoress for the second half of 1990.

We finish with two aerial photographs of today's Milford Haven (early 1999). This shows the 'new town' with its parallel streets in the foreground; the Marina (Milford Docks) dominates centre stage and Hakin is in the background. The second (opposite) taken from the Haven, shows more of Hakin, but concentrates on the Marina. The new Hakin Bridge and the Haven's Head Business Park are in the background. Marina development is impressive when it is remembered that in the late 1980s it was a derelict industrial lot.

Most importantly, these photographs serve to underline that the ups and downs in the well-being of Milford Haven always have and always will be inextricably linked with Milford Docks and the Waterway. Planners will hopefully also succeed in bringing much needed jobs by other means; but, the firm foundations of longer term economic success will always lie in the sensitive exploitation of the Town–Docks–Waterway relationship.

Acknowledgements

Most of the material we have used was drawn from Milford Haven Museum Archives. This comprehensive pictorial record, assembled over two decades, owes much to seperate collections presented to the museum by: The Milford Docks Company, Milford Haven Town Council, Gulf Oil, Royal Naval Armament Depot Milford Haven, *The Western Telegraph*, Frank Warburton (deceased) and Teddy Freeman (deceased). The compilers are grateful to the Trust of the Milford Haven Museum for allowing unfettered access to this material.

Special thanks go the the National Museum of Wales, Cardiff, for allowing us to use copies of an oil painting and watercolour depicting the early history of the Waterway and Town. Both the Pembrokeshire County Museum and Tenby Museum have been extremely helpful. It has been a pleasure to work with Tempus Publishing.

Many local people and groups helped with private photographs and advice including: Kevin McCauley (who also provided photographic copies), Joe Mayne, Eric White, Dorothy Miller, George Layton, Ray Evans, Ray Harding, Charlie Best, Pearl King, Stephen Griffith, Margaret Smith, Vilma Warr, Kenny Prickett, Bob Rickard (who also provided the artwork), John Springer, Ray Bowen and Morgan Howells.

Staff from the Milford Haven Police and Fire Stations helped, as did TARMAC (builders of the new bridge), the Docks Company, Gulf Oil, Elf Acquitaine and Texaco. A special thanks goes to all the voluntary helpers at the Milford Haven Museum, expecially to Kevin McCauley (photographer), Bob Rickard (artist), Anne Rimmer, Dilys McKay and Moyra Gee (administrative support), Eric Roberts (research and proof work) and Ray Harding (fisheries expert). There is always a danger in compiling long 'thank you' lists. You risk missing someone! If guilty, we apologise.

Finally, we hope our efforts will give pleasure to many, and we appeal to those readers who have better pictures of this exiting story to show them to the Milford Haven Museum and allow copies to be made for preservation in their archives.